I0654108

The Little Book of FARTs

Steven Appleby

BLOOMSBURY

Very special thanks to
Kerry Shale
who suggested this sophisticated and philosophical little volume

First published in Great Britain 2006

Copyright © 2006 by Steven Appleby

The moral right of the author has been asserted

Bloomsbury Publishing Plc, 36 Soho Square, London W1D 3QY

A CIP catalogue record for this book is available from the British Library

ISBN 0 7475 8245 9

ISBN-13 9780747582458

10 9 8 7 6 5 4 3 2 1

Printed in China by WKT Company Ltd

All papers used by Bloomsbury Publishing are natural, recyclable products made from wood grown in well-managed forests. The manufacturing processes conform to the environmental regulations of the country of origin.

www.bloomsbury.com/stevenappleby

www.stevenappleby.com

For
Stanley, who finds it very amusing,
Clement, who is an expert,
Jasper, who smiles wryly,
Alfred, who is too old for it now,
Thomas, who isn't,
and everyone else,
who has to put up with it

BLAT!

WHUMPH!

waft...

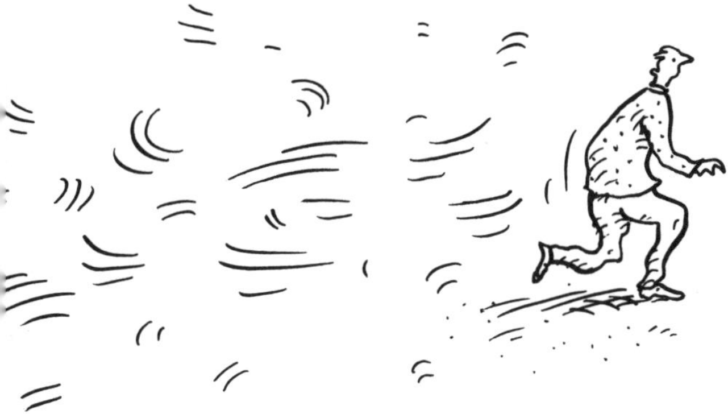

"FRAAPPPPP..."

Psst!

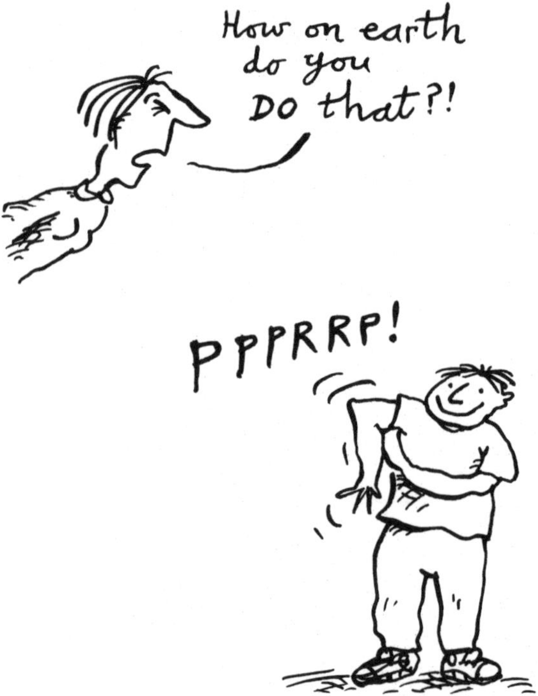
How on earth do you DO that?!
PPPRRP!

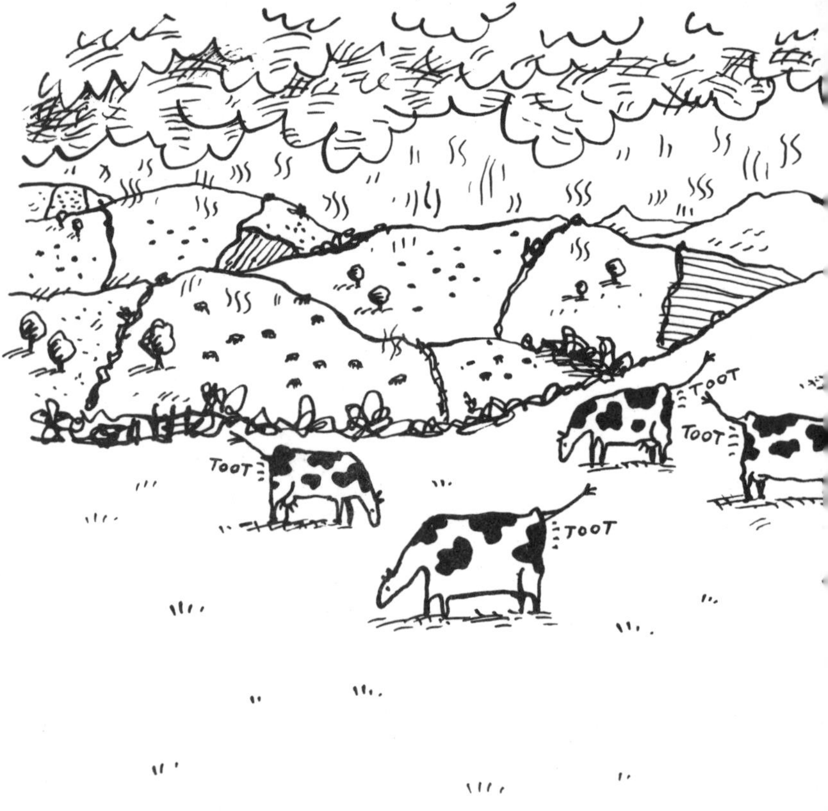
TOOT
TOOT
TOOT
TOOT

AN APRÈS CURRY FART

Broop!

A GERMAN FART

ANOTHER GERMAN FART

FARTING FOR FUN & PROFIT!

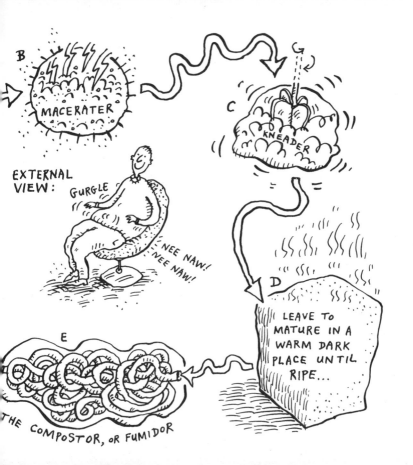

A FART COLLECTOR

SOME FART-COLLECTING EQUIPMENT FOR THE HOBBYIST

A FART-COLLECTING CHAIR

A FART-HARVESTING BAG (WITH REUSABLE TUBE)

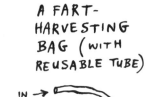

IN →

SPECIAL FART-INHALING BLOTTERS

fig a:

fig b:

COLLECTOR'S ITEM:

THIS DRESSING ROOM
CHAIR HAS ABSORBED THE
FARTS OF FAMOUS ACTORS,
INCLUDING SIR NOEL COWARD

WHY NOT BUILD UP YOUR OWN
COLLECTION OF FAMOUS FARTS
TO SELL ON EBAY?

ASK CELEBRITIES TO FART
ONTO THESE SPECIALLY
ABSORBENT PAGES

FART RECEPTIVE ZONE

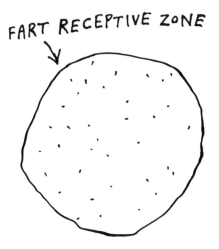

NAME _ _ _ _ _ _ _ _ _

SIGNATURE _ _ _ _ _ _ _

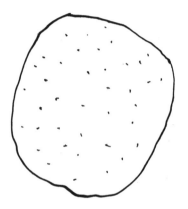

NAME _ _ _ _ _ _ _ _ _

SIGNATURE _ _ _ _ _ _ _ _

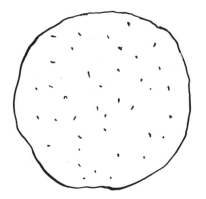

NAME _ _ _ _ _ _ _ _ _

SIGNATURE _ _ _ _ _ _ _

The Author
(old fart)